KT-168-458

Contents

NORWICH CITY COLLEGE LIBRARY

Stock No.	199701	
Class	796.087 KER —	
Cat.	SSA	Proc.	3WkL

LEARNING
SUPPORT
SERVICES

Please return
on or before
the last date
stamped below

City College
NORWICH

1 3 IIII 2005

3 1 MAR 2010

A FINE WILL BE CHARGED FOR OVERDUE ITEMS

199 701

sports coach
UK
The National Coaching Foundation

how to coach disabled people in sport

Copyright © **sports coach UK**, 2003

Reprinted October 2003

This document is copyright under the Berne Convention. All rights are reserved. Apart from any fair dealing for the purposes of private study, research, criticism or review, as permitted under the Copyright, Designs and Patents Act, 1988, no part of this publication may be reproduced, stored in a retrieval system, or transmitted in any form or by any means, electronic, electrical, chemical, mechanical, optical, photocopying, recording or otherwise, without the prior written permission of the copyright owner. Enquiries should be addressed to **Coachwise Solutions**.

ISBN 1 902523 54 7

Based on material from *Working with Disabled Sportspeople* (second edition)
© The National Coaching Foundation, 1991 (ISBN 0 947850 79 1)

Authors: Annie Kerr and Ian Stafford
Editor: Laura Graham
Sub-editor: Helen Bushell
Designer: Sandra Flintham
Cover photo courtesy of actionplus sports images
All other photos courtesy of **sports coach UK** and actionplus sports images
sports coach UK would like to thank Ken Black for the use of the Inclusion Spectrum

Published on behalf of
sports coach UK by

sports coach UK
114 Cardigan Road
Headingley
Leeds LS6 3BJ
Tel: 0113-274 4802 Fax: 0113-275 5019
E-mail: coaching@sportscoachuk.org
Website: www.sportscoachuk.org

Patron: HRH The Princess Royal

Coachwise Solutions
Coachwise Ltd
Chelsea Close
Off Amberley Road
Armley
Leeds LS12 4HP
Tel: 0113-231 1310 Fax: 0113-231 9606
E-mail: enquiries@coachwisesolutions.co.uk
Website: www.coachwisesolutions.co.uk

Introduction

You do not necessarily need special training to work with disabled people in sport. What you do need is sport-specific knowledge and skills, combined with the confidence and understanding to make any appropriate adjustments to the ways in which you already work in your own sport. As with all activities related to teaching, coaching and instructing, this knowledge will be most effective when you really get to know the individuals you are working with.

You may have a number of questions about how you can involve disabled participants in your coaching sessions or set up coaching sessions specifically for disabled people. This resource aims to answer the following questions:

- Who are disabled people in sport?

- How do I communicate effectively?

- How can disabled people participate in sport?

- What do coaches need to know?

- How can coaching be adapted or modified?

- What about safety issues?

- What about competition?

- Where next?

You will learn how, through appropriate planning and perhaps making minor adjustments to the way you work, you can be more effective when you work with disabled people. Working alongside participants with a disability, whether you are a coach, sports leader, development officer or volunteer, will simply be another challenge to your skills of observing and adapting.

> **All good coaches and teachers coach people, not sport.**

- To benefit fully from the content of this resource, you are strongly advised to attend the **sports coach UK (scUK)** workshop *How to Coach Disabled People in Sport*. This resource can then be used, for example, alongside the coaching programme of your national governing body (NGB) or local sports development programme, as well as other **scUK** workshops. It is strongly recommended that you try putting what you learn into practice, before attending the **scUK** workshop *Coaching Disabled People*.

- Throughout this pack, the pronouns he, she, him, her and so on are interchangeable and intended to be inclusive of both males and females. It is important in sport, as elsewhere, that both genders have equal status and opportunities.

- The issues covered in this resource will be of equal importance whether you are introducing individuals to a sport for the first time, or coaching experienced international competitors. Although the emphasis is on coaching, it is aimed at all those who lead or deliver sports programmes (eg coaches, leaders, teachers, instructors, development officers, officials, administrators, volunteers, parents/carers) and those with responsibility for the organisation of children's sport (eg national governing bodies, local authorities, centre managers, sports clubs).

Who are disabled people in sport?

First and foremost, people in sport are people. Like any other participant, they have individual needs and aspirations. To be an effective coach you need to get to know your participants and work with them to find suitable ways for them to get the most out of your sport.

The term *disabled people* is used throughout this resource. It is a generic term for anyone with a physical or sensory impairment, or learning disability. It is suggested that you use this term for any participants you coach who happen to have disabilities, unless they have a preference for another term. The language in this resource is acceptable to the majority of disabled people but if you are uncertain about which terminology to use, find out from the disabled people you coach. They will tell you what is acceptable and comfortable for them.

Disabled people have rejected some definitions of disability because they are formulated from a medical point of view. They are based on a *medical* or *individual* model of disability that tends to focus on what a person cannot do and attribute this to the individual's impairment. An alternative model, known as the *social* model of disability, focuses instead on how the environment, social systems and people's attitudes prevent disabled people from doing something.

According to the social model, a participant using a wheelchair, who cannot get into a fitness suite because it is only accessible via steps, is prevented from entering the facility by the lack of ramped access, not his impaired mobility. A participant who is not allowed to use a local swimming pool because she has a learning disability, and at times makes a lot of noise, is prevented by the attitudes of the people who stop her using the pool, not by her learning difficulty.

3

> **Disabled people cannot change but society can.**

People live, work and take part in sport in an environment that is often designed for non-disabled people. When you are coaching disabled people, try to think about what they can do rather than the medical label for their condition; you will be more likely to develop helpful coaching strategies and encourage an inclusive and welcoming introduction to sport.

sports coach UK

How do I communicate effectively?

If you are meeting a disabled person for the first time, you may wonder how to behave. Being told to 'behave normally' is not always a lot of help. There are a few practical tips in this section that will help you when meeting someone with a disability. Remember however, that the best approach is to check with each individual how they would like to communicate and use the common courtesy that you would with any participant.

In conversation, talk normally and don't *talk down* or talk to a third person as if the disabled person isn't there. Try to use language that is sensitive, appropriate and relevant. Generally speaking, it is best to avoid using terms such as 'you poor thing' or 'aren't you brave' as this can be patronising and offensive. Remember that everybody has the right to choose how they wish to be referred to and not everyone may choose to be referred to in the same way. If participants refer to themselves in a way you find offensive, you don't have to use the word just because they do.

When you first meet a disabled sports person, find out the best way to communicate with them. The following pages can be used as basic guidelines.

Coaching deaf or hearing impaired people

Remember that most hearing impaired people do have some hearing. First of all you need to determine how the person would like to communicate. They may prefer to lip-read or perhaps need an interpreter. For the people who have no hearing at all their principal language is often British Sign Language, which is a system of communication incorporating the fingers and hands to spell words.

Practical tips

When communicating with deaf or hearing impaired people, remember the following:

- Stand still and face participants with any light shining on your own face so they can see you clearly. Talk to the participant and not to the interpreter.

- Speak slowly and clearly; do not overemphasise words, shout, chew or cover your mouth when speaking.

- Some British Sign Language is useful but most instructions can be given simply with written instructions (dry wipe marker boards or chalkboards may be useful), gestures and demonstrations.

- To attract eye contact, either wave your hand or tap the person on the shoulder. Use similar visual clues to support instructions.

- Ensure that you give appropriate instructions before an activity begins and keep everyone involved by explaining any comments, questions or jokes made by group members.

- Check that participants understand and are not just copying you.

Coaching people who have difficulties with speech

Some participants' spoken language may be unclear or they may not use speech as a means of communication. These people may not necessarily be deaf or have a learning disability.

Practical tips

When communicating with people who have difficulties with speech, you should:

- be patient – don't rush them or finish their sentences
- always ensure you understand what the person has said before proceeding
- ask people, if in doubt, to repeat what they have said or write it down.

7

sports coach UK

Coaching blind or visually impaired people

Most visually impaired people have some sight. Find out initially what participants can see and how clearly they see things. Identify what lighting levels, contrasts between light and dark and times of the day are best for them to work in. Also, determine what shapes, colours and movements are easiest for them to see.

Practical tips

When working with blind or visually impaired people remember the following:

- Use the person's name to gain attention.

- Use clear, accurate verbal instructions and check for understanding.

- Make sure the participant knows when you have finished and you are moving away from them.

- Make sure the area in which you are working is kept free of obstacles and clutter.

- Supply any written information in a suitable format such as audio tape, large print or Braille copy.

You should help participants to familiarise themselves with the coaching environment by telling them:

- who is with them
- the layout of the area they are working in
- the location of key facilities, equipment, exits and potential hazards
- about any changes.

You can give a sense of direction by using:

- sound (eg voices can indicate where everyone is standing)
- touch (eg the distance from bowl to jack)
- familiar units (eg use the clock face by asking the participant to walk towards 10 o'clock or units of standard measurement by telling participants an object is 10 metres away)
- manual guidance (eg guide and support instruction by walking someone round a working area).

When leading a person who is blind, ask their advice. Most blind people prefer to be led by holding the guide's elbow while walking half a step behind; this gives information about direction and slope. You should also give verbal instructions about obstacles, changes in terrain/environment and people (eg whether doors open inwards or outwards, whether steps go up or down or whether you are entering a crowded area).

actionplus

Coaching people with a learning disability

People with a learning disability may find difficulty in learning some skills to the same level or at the same speed as their peers. The level of success will be unique to each individual and you should not make assumptions about an individual's ability.

Practical tips

- For any specific information, ask the participant. Sometimes people with a learning disability may be unable to supply this information themselves – it may then be appropriate to speak to a parent or guardian.

- Treat people by their age, not by their apparent level of ability.

- Use simple, straightforward language. Use gestures and changes in the volume or tone of your voice to draw attention to what you say.

- Use demonstrations given by yourself or other participants.

- Check the person understands and is not merely copying the demonstration (eg ask 'What should you do now?' rather than 'Have you understood?').

- Give time for skills to develop and repeat them often and in a variety of ways.

- Break skills down into easily learned steps.

Coaching people with a physical impairment

In general, communicating with people with a physical impairment is exactly the same as with any other person.

Practical tips
- Some wheelchair users consider their chairs to be part of their personal space so you should avoid touching or resting on the wheelchair, as you would avoid touching or resting on an individual.
- When talking to a wheelchair user, do so from a position that is comfortable for both of you – sitting on a chair at the same eye level as the other person is often the simplest way.
- If you are required to help push someone's wheelchair, ask him how he would like you to do this.

actionplus

What are the different ways disabled people can participate in sport?

There are many ways in which disabled people can be involved in sport. Sometimes disabled participants want to take part in activities with other disabled participants and sometimes, they may choose to take part in activities with non-disabled participants. How disabled people take part in an activity will depend upon their own motivation, the type of activity, their skill and fitness levels and how the activity can be modified and adapted.

The Inclusion Spectrum

There have been many attempts to produce a model that can help disabled people to be involved in sports activities in ways that suit them as individuals. The Inclusion Spectrum is an activity-based model that can contribute to the inclusion of disabled participants into sports sessions. It focuses on ability rather than disability.

The Inclusion Spectrum consists of five approaches to the delivery of physical activity programmes, ranging from fully open activities to totally segregated participation. Each approach aims to encourage and empower disabled and non-disabled people, in order to enhance the quality of their involvement.

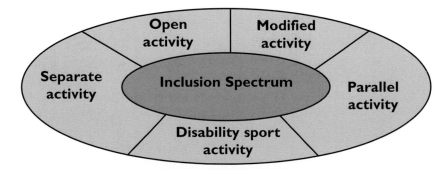

Figure 1: The Inclusion Spectrum

Open activities

In open activities everyone does the same thing without adaptation or modification, regardless of impairment. For example, deaf swimmers doing exactly the same training schedule as non-disabled swimmers during a session.

Modified activities

In modified activities everyone does the same task but with changes to rules, areas or equipment. For example, in tennis allowing people with mobility difficulties an extra bounce before having to return the ball.

Parallel activities

In parallel activities, everyone participates in the same type of activity, but different groups participate in different ways and at different levels. Participants can be grouped according to skill, fitness or the way in which they play the game.

For example, a group of participants can be split into three smaller groups for a ball passing game such as netball. The rules, equipment and playing area can be different in all three groups to suit the requirements of the group that is playing.

Disability sport activities

In these activities a group of non-disabled participants take part in an activity that has a disability sport focus; this is reverse integration. For example, non-disabled players can join in with a game of basketball that has been adapted and modified to meet the needs and abilities of the disabled players in the group.

Separate activities

These are activities in which participants play separately, either as individuals or in teams. This could happen, for example, when a group of disabled players practice together as a team preparing for a volleyball or tennis competition that has adapted rules to suit the needs and abilities of the individuals playing.

13

The facility that disabled people use for their sport may be solely for their use, reserved for their use or shared with non-disabled people but must always be accessible. The right way to include disabled people is also determined by the level at which a person chooses to participate. Find out whether they wish to:

- learn a new skill or sport
- take part in a recreational or social activity
- improve performance
- compete.

actionplus

Practical tips

- To determine the best coaching and activity programme, discuss with the disabled people you coach the various choices available.

- You should be careful to avoid assuming that sport for disabled people is only about therapy.

- The majority of disabled people want to use the same sports facilities and access the same opportunities as everyone else.

- Remember that many disabled people in sport have aspirations to reach the highest levels of international competition.

Where next?

Further information on coaching is provided in **sports coach UK**'s resource *What is Sports Coaching?*.[1]

14

---

1   Available from **Coachwise 1st4sport** (tel 0113-201 5555 or visit www.1st4sport.com).

What do coaches need to know?

As in all coaching, to work effectively with disabled people, you must meet their specific needs and aspirations in sport by recognising them as individuals. The following questions are some that you may need to discuss with your participants – not all will be necessary and you may think of others. They are actually applicable to all athletes and should become part of your standard practice when meeting a new performer you are about to coach.

What is your present skill level and what activities have you participated in previously?

You should always confirm skill level before starting a programme. Do not assume participants are beginners and remember that skills learned in one sport are often valuable in another.

What is your current level of fitness?

The answer to the first question may give you some clues as to how active the person has been in the past and what their current participation rate is. The response to this question should help you assess the individual's current physical condition – especially if you probe further by asking about the frequency and intensity of training and competing, past and present.

How often will you be coming to sessions and do you have any transport issues?

For many disabled people, this may not be a matter of choice but may be limited by factors such as access to transport, availability of a personal assistant or finance. The response will determine the length and intensity of sessions.

Have you used any modifications or adaptations in the past?

Why reinvent the wheel? Discuss with the participant what has been tried in the past (eg you may have previously modified a programme for a non-disabled performer who has become injured and might want to use a similar method). Don't discount things that failed previously without first trying to find out why they were unsuccessful.

Will you require any specialised equipment or particular assistance for the coaching programme?

Discuss with the participant whether any particular equipment will be needed which could range from a brightly coloured ball to a sports wheelchair. If such equipment is needed, you must ensure it is available. You must also be aware of any support given to the individual, whether it is from a personal assistant, parent or guardian, or other member of the group. The

responsibilities and procedures of the coaching session can then be explained to these people.

Do you have any previous or existing health considerations I need to be aware of?

This will be the same for any participant. It is important to emphasise that the information people give you will be treated with strict confidence and is only necessary to ensure you provide a safe and comfortable programme.

Do you have any other specific needs and interests I ought to be aware of?

This is a chance for the individual to explain any other issues that they feel may impact on their participation and performance in the sport. For example, it will be useful for you to have information about how an individual communicates (eg by using sign language or with the help of a hearing aid). Again, it should be emphasised that this information is necessary to ensure you provide an appropriate programme and environment.

Once you have gathered all the relevant information you should set realistic and challenging goals for the coaching programme in partnership with the participants. Consider modifications and adaptations to schedules, equipment and rules as necessary (eg hearing impaired swimmers may have a light attached to the side of their starting block rather than a starting gun).

While the information you need to gather from disabled participants will be the same for all participants, your approach and the way in which you use the information may need to be modified. Remember that some people may not wish to discuss the cause of an impairment; if people do wish to discuss the cause, they will tell you.

sports coach UK

How can coaching be adapted or modified?

Activities should be adapted in various ways to encourage and enable all participants to be included and to benefit. You have already been introduced to the social model of disability on page 3 and the Inclusion Spectrum on page 12. This section looks at how you can use both of these models to help you adapt and modify activities.

As outlined earlier, by referring to disability using a medical model, it may be wrongly assumed that a participant is unable to do an activity because their impairment prevents them. However, the real barriers to participation may be more to do with the environment, existing rules or procedures, lack of knowledge or skills on the part of people running the sport or an unwillingness of the person leading the activity to adapt and modify as appropriate.

A rounders player may find it difficult to play because she is unable to hit a moving ball effectively. Using a medical model, her visual impairment is hindering her performance but using a social model, it could be explained that the activity has not been adapted to suit the participant's ability. Placing the ball on a tee should make it easier to hit.

Ways to modify or adapt activities

Adaptations and modifications always involve some or all of the following principles:

Space

Task

Equipment

Position

Speed

Space

- Play the game at floor level.
- Adjust the size of the playing area.
- Vary the distance that needs to be covered (bearing in mind that being closer to a partner when catching or passing allows less response time).
- Vary the height of the net (lowering nets also means less time to respond).
- Vary the size of the target area.
- Allow players to move either nearer or further away from opposition players.
- Let players start at different places.
- Mark off individual player's areas with hoops.

Task

- Make the game easier or harder by altering some of the rules.
- Make sure players try a number of different roles or positions.
- Allow players to play in different ways (eg seated on the floor).

- Alter the ways to score.
- Set open-ended challenges so participants can achieve at their own level (eg find the most effective way to send the ball to your partner).

Equipment

Consider the following aspects:

- Weight
- Texture
- Colour
- Size or length
- Shape

You could adopt multicoloured foam balls, lighter bats with larger heads and shorter handles or specialised equipment such as a tee stand for hitting a stationary ball in a rounders game.

Position

- Practise the action (eg catching a ball) standing still at first and then introduce increases in movement and speed.
- Make sure player position is suitable to the individual and activity.

- Make sure visually impaired players can orientate themselves.

Speed

- Vary the speed of the object thrown or use a slower moving object such as a beach ball.

- Use a tee stand so the ball is hit from a static position.

- Allow slow movements.

- Alter the speed of play to suit the individual players (eg heighten the net to give receivers more time to respond or change rules to allow one or two bounces).

sports coach UK

Practical tips

The following examples show how sports are adapted to include disabled people:

- **Table Tennis**
  Adapt the skills to enable a one-hand serve.

- **Lawn Tennis**
  Modify the rules of competition by allowing the ball to bounce twice for wheelchair users.

- **Volleyball**
  Alter the distance and areas of play, and allow a player to serve from a point closer to the net.

- **Cricket**
  Modify or use alternative equipment such as large brightly coloured balls for visually impaired participants or balls which contain a bell for blind players.

- **Archery**
  Give simple touch reference points for feet and hands to enable visually impaired or blind archers to line up accurately with the target.

Equipment

For some sports, specific equipment such as a mono-ski is sometimes necessary, although for general sport participation it is not required. As skills develop, specific equipment, such as a sports wheelchair or flex-foot for a participant who has had a lower limb amputation, can help enhance performance. For more information, contact the appropriate disability sports organisation (contact details on pages 29–31).

actionplus

What about safety issues?

The basic principles required to ensure safe practice within your sport are the same for all participants. However, the law requires that an extra duty of care is needed when coaching disabled people. Coaches should follow good coaching practice and always manage risks at a level that is reasonably acceptable for the sport. It is important to assess the risks with the individual participant concerned – if in doubt, contact your sport's national governing body (NGB).

Insurance

All coaches should have public liability insurance and should ensure this includes coaching disabled participants. If you are unsure, talk to your NGB or the English Federation for Disability Sport (EFDS).

First aid

Make sure you know where to find the first aid kit or first-aiders. Where possible, you should carry your own basic first aid kit (eg bandages/ strapping, antiseptic solution, re-usable ice pack, dressings for wounds or grazes). You could also benefit from gaining a first aid qualification from organisations such as the Red Cross or St John Ambulance.

Safe surfaces

Although surfaces such as grass may be safe playing areas for non-disabled people, these can present difficulties for wheelchair users or participants using walking aids. If you have any doubts check with the participant.

Medical issues

It is always good practice for coaches to be aware of relevant health information about all their participants. As with anyone you coach, you should find out any relevant medical information, in the first instance, from the individual concerned. If still unsure, you may have to consult with others. Also, you should be applying the general principle of good practice by constantly observing how individuals respond to the activities within your coaching programme.

Some health issues will be the same for disabled and non-disabled participants (eg diet or intensity of an exercise programme) and other issues might arise because of an individual's particular impairment (eg a performer with Paraplegia). These could influence specific activity considerations for that individual (eg the risk of damage to the skin tissue for someone with reduced skin sensitivity in physical contact activities).

Wheelchair users

Remember that when you coach participants who are wheelchair users in an active sport, you must ensure they propel their chairs as effectively as possible. This may need to be given a high priority within their coaching programmes. Since there is now a wide range of different wheelchairs available, often specifically designed for the sport, you should seek advice from experienced wheelchair users. Find out information such as how people propel their wheelchair while still holding a racket.

It is useful to be aware that some physically disabled participants may have reduced or impaired cardiovascular function that may increase their susceptibility to heat or cold. They may also have a lack of skin sensation that could lead to a greater risk from accidental injury to skin and soft tissue.

Lifting

On occasions, it may be necessary to transfer or lift disabled persons so they can access the sporting environment; such actions are the subject of European regulations. The managers of the sports facilities you use or your NGB should be aware of the appropriate guidance and training required. For the safety of both yourself and your participants you should find out further information from either your NGB or one of the various disability sport organisations listed in the **Where next?** section (page 26).

Emergency evacuation

- **General**

  You and the participants must be aware of the emergency evacuation procedures for any facility in which you are working. Be familiar with the design of the building and assess emergency procedures, giving consideration to any which relate specifically to disabled people. It is also important to:

  - check all exit routes

  - identify assembly areas for wheelchair users.

- **People with learning disabilities**

  It may be important to observe closely participants with a learning disability within the coaching environment. They may be less aware of the safety precautions, accepted rules of behaviour around the sports arena and evacuation procedures. Identify a partner who will assist a participant with a learning disability in the event of an emergency evacuation.

- **Participants with sensory disabilities**

  People with a hearing impairment may not hear fire alarms or messages over public address systems. Some facilities have flashing lights accompanying their alarm systems. If the facility does not have this system, you must identify a hearing person who will communicate important information about evacuation to hearing impaired or deaf participants. You should also allocate a partner to assist with visually impaired or blind participants should they need to leave the building in an emergency.

Where next?

Further information on safety issues is provided in **sports coach UK**'s resource *How to Coach Sports Safely.*[1]

---

1   Available from **Coachwise 1st4sport** (tel 0113-201 5555 or visit www.1st4sport.com).

What about competition?

Just like other individuals in sport, disabled people may want to compete on a variety of levels from social and recreational to club representative and international competition. The coach of a disabled participant should be aware of the various competitive opportunities that may be available and discuss these, as appropriate, with the participant.

Disabled people can choose to compete against other disabled people or non-disabled peers. Disability sport agencies organise events exclusively for disabled people such as National Championships. If the choice is to compete against non-disabled peers, it is important to check that any adapted or specialist equipment is permitted within the competition rules.

Are there different rules?

You will probably be aware of the rules governing your sport in open competition. However, the rules for disability sport events may be different. To enable participants to compete against people with a similar impairment, many of these events use classification or profile systems. Generally, all participants competing will need to have been given the correct classification or profile number before entering an event. You will need to discuss this with the individual or talk to the appropriate disability sports organisation.

In a number of sports, there may also be different rules of competition for disabled participants. Some of these have been mentioned earlier in this resource (eg adapting table tennis for a one-handed serve) but there are others to be considered. For example, the weight of throwing implements may differ from those used in NGB competitions. For more information, contact your NGB or the relevant disability sports organisation.

Where next?

The information in this study pack should have given you the encouragement and confidence to work with disabled people. You should be aware of communication issues in sport and recognise the range of participation opportunities identified within the Inclusion Spectrum. Some useful principles and practical coaching strategies have been outlined along with information on competition. Your confidence will increase as your experience grows and with this confidence you will soon be able to deliver the technical aspects of your sport to disabled participants.

Although most disabled people are generally involved in a variety of activities as participants, they can also be involved as coaches, officials and administrators. If you are a disabled participant why not consider becoming involved in another way such as coaching or sports leadership? If you are non-disabled, please encourage disabled people to become involved in other ways.

There are various routes into sports coaching. In the first instance, disabled people can gain appropriate qualifications in sports coaching by following approved NGB courses. Anyone interested in becoming a coach can obtain a fact sheet from the **sports coach UK (scUK)**

Information Service. (See page 29 for contact details and please enclose SAE.)

scUK offers a variety of workshops and resources related to coaching disabled performers.

Workshops

- Coaching Disabled Performers
- How to Coach Disabled People in Sport

For more information about these workshops, contact your nearest Regional Training Unit (RTU). RTU contact details are available from **scUK** (tel 0113-274 4802 or visit www.sportscoachuk.org).

Resources

- DePauw, K and Gavron, S (1995) **Disability and sport**. Champaign IL, Human Kinetics. ISBN 0 87322 484 0.[1]

- Jowsey, S (1992) **Can I play too? Physical education for physically disabled children in mainstream schools**. London, David Foulton. ISBN 1 85346 217 9.

- Latto, K and Norrice, B (1989) **Give us the chance – sport and physical recreation with people with a mental handicap**. London, Disabled Living Foundation. No longer in print.

- Palfreyman, T (1994) **Designing for accessibility**. London, Centre for Accessible Environments. ISBN 0 90397 623 4.

- PE for All Group and British Sports Association for the Disabled (1992) **Physical education and disability**.[2]

- Royal National Institute for the Blind (1996) **Looming into PE: guidelines for teaching PE to children with visual impairment**. London, RNIB. ISBN 1 80901 206 6.[3]

- Webber, A (1991) **Sport and mobility**. Produced in association with the Royal Association for Disability and Rehabilitation. Dunstable, Folens Publishing. ISBN 1 852762 75 X.

---

1   Available from **Coachwise 1st4sport** (tel 0113-201 5555 or visit www.1st4sport.com).

2   Available from **Coachwise 1st4sport** (tel 0113-201 5555 or visit www.1st4sport.com).

3   Available from the RNIB (tel 020-7388 1266 or visit www.rnib.org.uk).

Other resources in the Coaching Essentials series[1] include:

What is Sports Coaching?
This new resource clearly defines coaching and introduces the basic components of coaching sessions. Including sections on the roles, responsibilities and qualities of a coach, it is an ideal introductory text for new and existing coaches. (Based on *The Coach In Action*.)

How to Coach Sports Safely
Focusing on safe practice in sport, this resource clearly outlines the health and safety issues associated with coaching. Includes new sections on managing risk and manual handling. Essential guidance for every coach. (Based on *Safety and Injury*.)

How to Coach Sports Effectively
This resource includes practical tips to help develop coaching skills and allow participants to get the most benefits from your sessions. Also features chapters on planning, organising and delivering sessions. Everything you need to be an effective coach. (Based on *Planning and Practice*.)

How to Coach Children in Sport
Aimed at anyone working with children in sport, this easy-to-read resource presents the basic principles of good practice and introduces the concept of long-term athlete development. (Based on *Working With Children*.)

---

1   Available from **Coachwise 1st4sport** (tel 0113-201 5555 or visit www.1st4sport.com).

Useful contacts

sports coach UK

sports coach UK works closely with sports governing bodies to provide a comprehensive service for coaches throughout the UK. This includes an extensive programme of workshops which have proved valuable to coaches from all types of sport and every level of experience. For details of **scUK** workshops in your area, contact your nearest Regional Training Unit. For regular updates on **scUK** workshops in your area, contact your nearest Regional Training Unit. For more information about **scUK's** workshops and other services, contact:

> **sports coach UK**
> 114 Cardigan Road
> Headingley
> Leeds LS6 3BJ
> Tel: 0113-274 4802
> Fax: 0113-275 5019
>
> **E-mail:**
> coaching@sportscoachuk.org
>
> **Website:**
> www.sportscoachuk.org

National governing bodies

The national governing body for your sport or activity will give advice on coaching courses and other relevant information. Addresses of governing bodies are available from:

> **Central Council of Physical Recreation**
> Francis House
> Francis Street
> London SW1P 1DE
> Tel: 020-7854 8500
> Fax: 020-7854 8501
>
> **E-mail:**
> info@ccpr.org.uk
>
> **Website:**
> ww.ccpr.org.uk

Useful addresses of disability sports organisations

Besides the national governing bodies of sport, there are other types of organisations providing opportunities for disabled people – these are generally grouped as disability-specific or sport-specific.

British Amputee & Les Autres Sports Association (BALASA)
5 Bells Farm Close
Brandwood
Birmingham
B14 5QP
Tel: 0121-605 9549

British Blind Sport
4–6 Victoria Terrace
Leamington Spa
Warwickshire
CV31 3AB
Tel: 08700-789000
Fax: 08700-789001
E-mail:
info@britishblindsport.org.uk
www.britishblindsport.org.uk

British Deaf Sports Council
7A Bridge Street
Otley LS21 1BQ
Voice: 01943-850214
DCT: 01943-850081
Fax: 01943-850828

British Paralympic Association
Norwich Union Building
9th Floor
69 Park Lane
Croydon
Surrey
CR9 1BG
Tel: 020-7662 8882
Fax: 020-7662 8310
Website:
www.paralympics.org.uk

Disability Sport England
Unit 4G, N17 Studios
784–788 High Road
Tottenham
London
N17 0DA
Tel: 020-8801 4466
Fax: 020-8801 6644
E-mail: info@dse.org.uk
Website:
www.disabilitysport.org.uk

British Wheelchair Sports Foundation
Guttmann Road
Stoke Mandeville
Aylesbury
HP21 9PP
Tel: 01296-395995
Fax: 01296-424171
E-mail: enquiries@
britishwheelchairsports.org
Website:
www.britishwheelchairsports.org

Cerebral Palsy Sport
Suite 32, Trent Bridge Cricket
 Centre
Notts County Cricket Club Ltd
Trent Bridge
Nottingham NG2 6AG
Tel: 0115-982 5352 or
0115-982 5358
Fax: 0115-981 5484
E-mail: info@cpsport.org
Website: www.cpsport.org

Disability Sport Cymru
National Sports Centre for Wales
Sophia Gardens
Cardiff CF1 9SW
Tel: 029-2030 0525/6
Fax: 029-2030 0599

**English Federation of
Disability Sport**
Manchester Metropolitan
 University
Alsager Campus
Hassall Road, Alsager
Stoke on Trent ST7 2HL
Tel: 0161-247 5294
Fax: 0161-247 6895
E-mail: federation@efds.co.uk
Website: www.efds.net

**English Sports Association for
People with Learning Disability**
Unit 9, Milner Way
Ossett WF5 9JN
Tel: 01924-267555
Fax: 01924-267666
E-mail: info@esapld.co.uk
Website: www.esapld.co.uk

Friends of Young Deaf (FYD)
120a Abbet Street
Nuneaton
CV11 5BX
Tel: 024-7663 15017
Fax: 024-7664 1517
Minicom: 024-7632 8083

Scottish Disability Sport
FIPER Viewfield Road
Glenrothes
Fife KY6 2RA
Tel: 01592-415700
Fax: 01592-415710

**Special Olympics Great
Britain**
Lower Ground Floor
4 St Johns Road
Tunbridge Wells
Kent
TN14 9TP
Tel: 01892-540484
Fax: 01892-545247

**UK Sports Association for
People with Learning
Disability (UKSAPLD)**
Ground Floor
Leroy House
436 Essex Road
London N1 3QP
Tel: 020-7354 1030
Fax: 020-7354 2593
E-mail:
office@uksapld.freeserve.co.uk

31